Beginning Letters

Karen Bryant-Mole

Gareth Stevens Publishing
A WORLD ALMANAC EDUCATION GROUP COMPANY

Mortimer's Fun with Words

For a free color catalog describing Gareth Stevens' list of high-quality books and multimedia programs, call 1-800-542-2595 (USA) or 1-800-461-9120 (Canada). Gareth Stevens Publishing's Fax: (414) 332-3567.

Library of Congress Cataloging-in-Publication Data available upon request from publisher. Fax: (414) 332-3567 for the attention of the Publishing Records Department.

ISBN 0-8368-2746-5

This North American edition first published in 2000 by
Gareth Stevens Publishing
A World Almanac Education Group Company
330 West Olive Street, Suite 100
Milwaukee, WI 53212 USA

This edition © 2000 by Gareth Stevens, Inc. Original © BryantMole Books, 1999. First published in 1999 by Evans Brothers Limited, 2A Portman Mansions, Chiltern Street, London W1M 1LE, United Kingdom. Additional end matter © 2000 by Gareth Stevens, Inc.

Created by Karen Bryant-Mole
Photographs by Zul Mukhida
Designed by Jean Wheeler
Teddy bear by Merrythought Ltd.

Printed in the United States of America

1 2 3 4 5 6 7 8 9 04 03 02 01 00

contents

pl

Mortimer is eating a plum.

The word **plum** begins with the letters **pl**.

Can you name these things that begin with the letters **pl**?

fl sl

Mortimer can play the flute.

The word **flute** begins with the letters **fl**.

Can you find two more things
that begin with the letters **fl**?

Can you find something that
begins with the letters **sl**?

gl cl

Mortimer is using paper and glue.

The word **glue** begins with the letters **gl**.

Can you find two more things that begin with the letters **gl**?

Can you find something that begins with the letters **cl**?

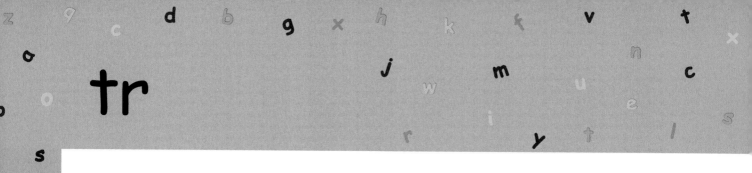

tr

Mortimer is playing with his train.

The word **train** begins with the letters **tr**.

Can you name these things that begin with the letters **tr**?

bl br fr

Mortimer has some blocks.

The word **block** begins with the letters **bl**.

Can you find two things that begin with the letters **br**?

Can you find something that begins with the letters **fr**?

cr pr

Mortimer is playing with a toy crane.

The word **crane** begins with the letters **cr**.

Can you find two things that begin with the letters **cr**?

Can you find something that begins with the letters **pr**?

dr gr

Mortimer is looking at a dragon.

The word **dragon** begins with the letters **dr**.

16

Can you find two
things that begin
with the letters **dr**?

Can you find
something that begins
with the letters **gr**?

sc sk

Mortimer is standing next to a scarecrow.

The word **scarecrow** begins with the letters **sc**.

Can you find something that begins with the letters **sc**?

Can you find two things that begin with the letters **sk**?

sn st sp

Mortimer sees a snail.

The word **snail** begins with the letters **sn**.

Can you find another animal
that begins with the letters **sn**?

Can you find an animal that
begins with the letters **st**?

Can you find an
animal that begins
with the letters **sp**?

Mortimer has some jars of paint.

The color **blue** begins with the letters **bl**.

Can you find another color that begins with the letters **bl**?

Can you find two colors that begin with the letters **gr**?

glossary/index

crane — a machine with a tall swinging arm used to lift and move things from one place to another 14

dragon — a made-up monster that looks like a giant lizard, sometimes with wings 16

flute — a tube-shaped musical instrument that is played by blowing into or across a hole at one end 6

glue — gooey liquid used to hold or stick things together 8

plum — a type of fruit that grows on a tree, has a pit, and has purple, red, or yellow skin 4

scarecrow — a figure, made to look like a person, that is sometimes set up in a field to scare birds away from crops, such as corn 18

snail — an animal with a soft body and a hard, coiled shell that moves very slowly 20

train — a long line of railroad cars that carry people and things from one place to another 10

videos

Learn Phonics Letters. (Goodtimes Home Video)

Learn to Read with Phonics. (Goodtimes Home Video)

Rock 'N Learn – Letter Sounds. (Rock 'N Learn)